READING POWER

Working Together

Astronauts

Joanne Mattern

The Rosen Publishing Group's
PowerKids Press™
New York

Published in 2002 by The Rosen Publishing Group, Inc.
29 East 21st Street, New York, NY 10010

First Edition

Book Design: Laura Stein

Photo Credits: Front cover © Rob Atkins/Image Bank; pp. 4–5, 7, 8, 19 © Roger Ressmeyer/Corbis; pp. 6, 9, 21 © Photri/NASA; pp.10–11, 21 © NASA/Roger Ressmeyer/Corbis; p.13 © World Perspectives/Stone; pp.15, 17, 21, back cover © Photodisc

Mattern, Joanne, 1963–
Astronauts / by Joanne Mattern.
    p. cm. — (Working together)
Includes bibliographical references and index.
ISBN 0-8239-5977-5 (library binding)
1. Astronauts—Juvenile literature. 2. Astronautics—Juvenile
literature. [1. Astronauts. 2. Occupations.]   I. Title. II. Working
together (PowerKids Press)
TL793 .M377 2002
629.45'0092'2—dc21
                                          2001000551

Manufactured in the United States of America

Contents

Meet the Astronauts

These are astronauts. Astronauts work together in space.

Astronauts wear special suits when they go into space.

Astronauts train before they fly into space. Sometimes they train underwater in their space suits.

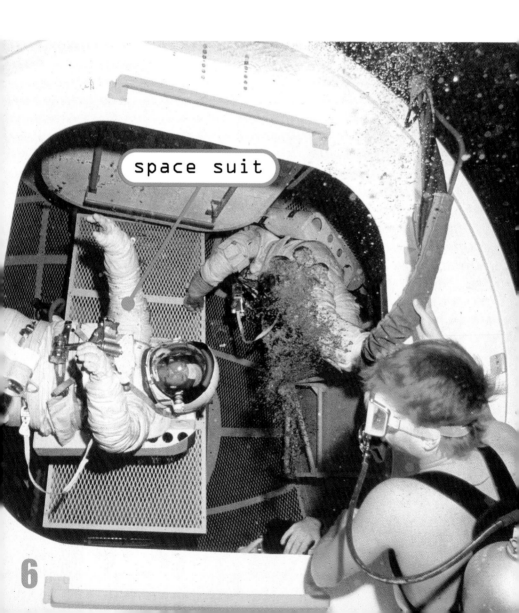

space suit

The astronauts fly into space on the space shuttle.

Life on the Space Shuttle

There is no gravity in space. The astronauts float in the space shuttle when they move from place to place.

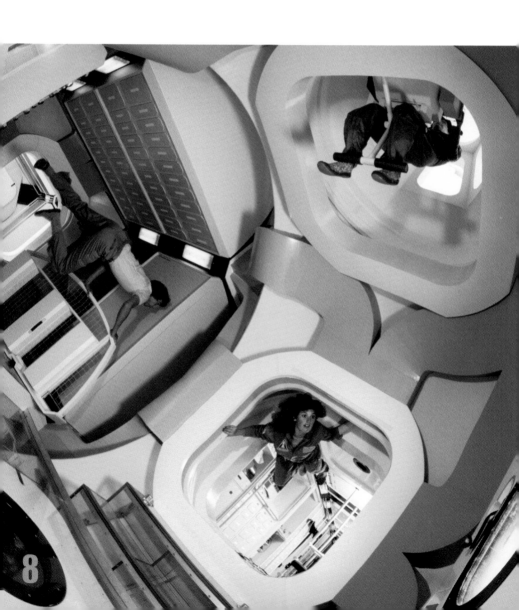

Astronauts have to strap themselves to a wall when they sleep.

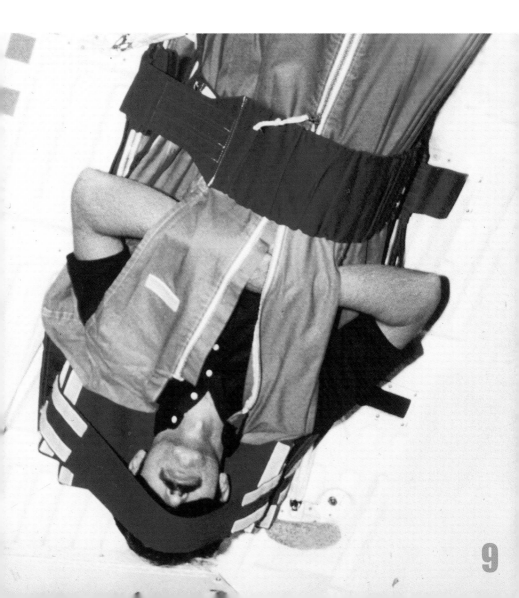

Astronauts eat food that comes in small bags. They have to eat food that doesn't crumble. Floating crumbs can hurt the computers in the space shuttle.

The Pilot

Some astronauts are pilots. Pilots use computers to fly the space shuttle.

computers

These astronauts work with special tools. Astronauts have to be careful not to let screws or other objects float into space. Floating objects can harm the space shuttle.

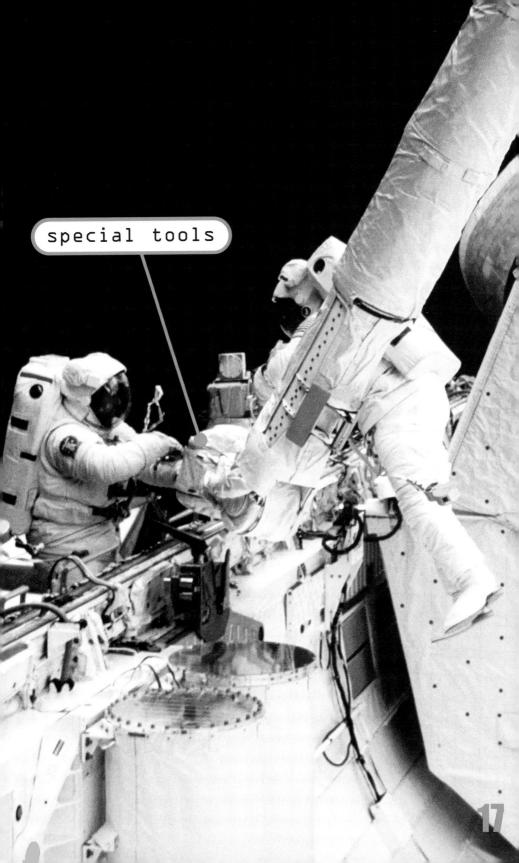

special tools

17

Astronauts keep records of everything they do in space. Scientists on Earth use these records to learn more about life in space.

Astronauts live and work far away from Earth. They have to work together to do their jobs well.

Glossary

astronauts (**as**-truh-nawts) members of the crew of a spacecraft

gravity (**grav**-uh-tee) the force that pulls things down and keeps them from floating away

pilots (**py**-luhtz) people trained to operate the controls of a spacecraft

records (**rehk**-uhrdz) something written down and kept for future use

satellite (**sat**-l-yt) an artificial object shot by a rocket into an orbit around Earth

space (**spays**) the region past Earth's atmosphere

space shuttle (**spays shuht**-l) a spacecraft with wings that can orbit Earth and land like an airplane

Resources

Books

Astronauts
by Tami Deedrick
Capstone Press (1998)

If You Were an Astronaut
by Virginia Schomp
Benchmark Books (1998)

Web Site

Work in Space
http://web.missouri.edu/~uawww/
 spaceday/work.htm

Index

Word Count: 200

Note to Librarians, Teachers, and Parents

If reading is a challenge, Reading Power is a solution! Reading Power is perfect for readers who want high-interest subject matter at an accessible reading level. These fact-filled, photo-illustrated books are designed for readers who want straightforward vocabulary, engaging topics, and a manageable reading experience. With clear picture/text correspondence, leveled Reading Power books put the reader in charge. Now readers have the power to get the information they want and the skills they need in a user-friendly format.